FRANKLIN D. ROOSEVELT

A Photo-Illustrated Biography
by Steve Potts

Bridgestone Books
an Imprint of Capstone Press

Facts about Franklin D. Roosevelt

• Franklin Delano Roosevelt was the 32nd president of the United States.

• He contracted polio and his legs were paralyzed.

• He was elected president four times.

• He served longer than any other president.

Bridgestone Books are published by Capstone Press • 818 North Willow Street, Mankato, Minnesota 56001
Copyright © 1996 by Capstone Press • All rights reserved • Printed in the United States of America

Library of Congress Cataloging-in-Publication Data
Potts, Steve, 1956-
    Franklin D. Roosevelt, a photo-illustrated biography/ by Steve Potts.
    p. cm.--(Read and discover photo-illustrated biographies)
    Includes bibliographical references and index.
    Summary: A brief biography of the thirty-second president of the United States.
    ISBN 1-56065-453-8
    1. Roosevelt, Franklin D. (Franklin Delano), 1882-1945--Juvenile literature. 2. Presidents--United
States--Biography--Juvenile literature. [1. Roosevelt, Franklin D. (Franklin Delano), 1882-1945. 2.
Presidents.] I. Title. II Series.
E807.P64 1996
973.917'092--dc20
[B]

                   95-44568
                     CIP
                      AC

Photo credits
Archive Photos, cover, 6, 10, 16.
FPG, 4, 8, 12, 14, 18, 20.

Table of Contents

Great President 5

School Years 7

Franklin and Eleanor 9

Cousin Teddy 11

Surviving Polio 13

Governor Roosevelt 15

The Great Depression 17

World War II 19

The President Is Dead 21

Words from Franklin D. Roosevelt 22

Important Dates in Franklin D. Roosevelt's Life 23

Words to Know 23

Read More 24

Useful Addresses and Internet Sites 24

Index 24

Words in **boldface** type in the text are defined in the Words to Know section in the back of this book.

Great President

Franklin Delano Roosevelt was one of the United States' greatest presidents. Few American presidents have done more for their country. He helped Americans survive the economic disaster of the Great Depression. He gave hope to millions with his radio speeches. He led Americans to victory in World War II. He made the United States a world power.

He served longer than any other president. And he governed from his wheelchair. He could not walk without help. His legs were paralyzed.

Franklin D. Roosevelt, often called FDR, was born on January 30, 1882. His parents were James Roosevelt and Sara Delano Roosevelt. He was born in Hyde Park, New York. It is a small town along the Hudson River.

No matter where FDR went, he always returned to his Hyde Park home. In April 1945, he came back for the final time. He is buried in the garden of the house he loved so much.

Franklin D. Roosevelt served longer than any other president.

School Years

In the 1890s, the children of wealthy families were educated by **tutors** and at private schools. FDR's parents took him to Europe in 1890. They brought along a tutor. She was a young Swiss girl named Jeanne Sandoz. She gave FDR a love for physics and chemistry. Her views on **politics** also influenced him. When she left Hyde Park in 1893, Arthur Dumper became FDR's tutor. Dumper loved athletics and nature. He was not only FDR's tutor. He also became his good friend.

When FDR was 14, he went to Groton School in Massachusetts. In 1900, he enrolled at Harvard University. FDR was not a brilliant student but he was popular. He belonged to several clubs and was editor of the student newspaper.

He ended his college career at Columbia University. He went to law school there for two years. FDR passed the New York bar exam, but he did not finish his degree.

Franklin posed with his parents, James and Sara Roosevelt, in 1899.

Franklin and Eleanor

Franklin married his distant cousin, Anna Eleanor Roosevelt, in 1905. Eleanor was the niece of President Teddy Roosevelt. She had a difficult life as a girl. Her parents died when she was young. It was not until she went to school in England that Eleanor began to enjoy life. She liked being with friends and family. But she did not enjoy social life and parties.

Eleanor wanted to have a life of her own beyond the usual duties of a politician's wife. She wanted to learn more about politics and current events. By the time FDR became president, Eleanor had a long record of helping people. She helped people of all ages and backgrounds.

As her husband became more active in politics, Eleanor raised their daughter and four sons. She and FDR called their children "the chicks." They were Anna, James, Elliott, Franklin Jr., and John. Eleanor led an active life inside and outside the home. She played a very important role in FDR's political career.

Franklin and Eleanor Roosevelt were married in 1905.

yond a pe

Cousin Teddy

FDR admired his cousin Teddy Roosevelt. As a young man, FDR tried to speak and act like his famous relative. In 1913, he got the chance to follow Teddy's path to Washington. FDR became the assistant secretary of the navy, just as Teddy had been.

FDR loved to sail and was very interested in naval affairs. His office walls were covered with pictures of old sailing ships. Some of his relatives had been ship captains.

Franklin's job gave him valuable experience running a large government department. When the United States entered World War I in 1917, FDR wanted to quit his job and join the military. But his boss would not let him. He was needed at his job. FDR felt he missed a chance to make a name for himself.

In 1920, the Democratic Party picked James M. Cox to run for president. The party picked FDR to run for vice president. The men lost to the Republican **candidates**. But FDR had made a name for himself throughout the country.

When he was assistant secretary of the navy, FDR, left, helped entertain the Prince of Wales, right.

Surviving Polio

Today it is rare to hear of Americans getting **polio.** There are medicines to prevent the disease. But until the mid-1950s, many people got polio. The disease paralyzed them and often killed them.

FDR got polio in August 1921. He was on vacation at his summer home on Campobello Island in New Brunswick, Canada. He became paralyzed from the waist down. FDR was determined to survive. He spent many hours doing exercises to keep his muscles strong. He found that swimming helped him rebuild his strength. In 1924, he went to Warm Springs, Georgia. The warm waters there helped him feel better.

FDR kept fighting. He was determined to get back into politics. After four years of treatments at Warm Springs, he returned to politics. He was elected governor of New York in 1928. But FDR was never strong again. He wore leg braces and used a cane. It was hard for him to stand or walk. He often used a wheelchair.

FDR wore leg braces and used a cane.

Governor Roosevelt

FDR hoped to use his office as governor to help New York's people. By the time he left office in 1933, he had improved rural education. He lowered taxes for small farmers. He used the state's water power to provide less expensive electricity. He improved conditions for workers. FDR also helped set up programs for old-age pensions and unemployment pay.

FDR liked being governor. But he wanted to return to Washington, D.C. The Great Depression was wrecking the economy. FDR wanted to help the country. He also thought he would be a better president than the one in office, Herbert Hoover.

In 1932, FDR ran for president. American voters elected him in a **landslide**. They hoped he could help the American economy recover. FDR was elected three more times, in 1936, 1940, and 1944. After that, Congress passed a law limiting a president to two four-year terms.

FDR was governor of New York before serving as president.

The Great Depression

When FDR took office in 1933, the United States was on the verge of economic collapse. The Great Depression was at its worst. It lasted from 1929 to 1939.

During his campaign, FDR talked about the ways he could help the American people. He met with experts in banking, agriculture, and business. He got their advice. FDR and his advisers created a plan to help America survive the Depression. They called it the New Deal.

During his first 100 days as president, FDR asked Congress to pass 15 major laws to help improve the economy. Congress passed them all. New programs for agriculture, banking, electrical power, and employment gave Americans hope. FDR further boosted their confidence with his fireside chats. These were radio speeches heard by millions of Americans. They reassured Americans that their president cared about them.

The New Deal ended in 1938. By that time, New Deal programs had touched almost every American's life.

Millions of Americans heard FDR's fireside chats on the radio.

World War II

FDR met his greatest challenge in World War II. He tried to keep the United States out of the war in Europe and Asia. But when the Japanese attacked Pearl Harbor on December 7, 1941, he had no choice. America was at war again for the second time in 25 years.

FDR managed a war on two **fronts**. Americans were fighting in Europe and in the Pacific. He helped plan military operations. He also had to get American businesses to produce things for the war. Car factories made jeeps and tanks. Shipyards made warships and submarines.

America was not producing enough food to feed its people. So FDR put food **rationing** into place. It worked.

FDR made friends with many world leaders. Winston Churchill was the British prime minister. He became one of FDR's best friends. FDR and Churchill wrote many letters to each other. They visited each other whenever they could.

FDR met with Winston Churchill, left, and Joseph Stalin in 1945 in Yalta to discuss the war.

The President Is Dead

By April 1945, the end of the war was near. American troops were crushing the German army. American planes were bombing Japan.

Running the war took a lot of energy. It created a lot of stress. Many people worried about FDR's health.

On April 12, 1945, FDR was sitting in the garden of his Warm Springs home. An artist was painting his picture. FDR's hands shook and he was pale. That afternoon, while signing some papers, FDR slumped over in his chair. Several hours later, he died.

His death was a tragedy for many people. FDR had been president for 12 years. Americans had come to depend on his hope for their future. They loved the man who worried so much about them.

As his funeral train moved north, thousands of people came to the railroad tracks to say goodbye. Franklin Delano Roosevelt was one of America's greatest presidents. He was going home to Hyde Park for the last time.

FDR is buried at Hyde Park, his family home.

Words from Franklin D. Roosevelt

"The only thing we have to fear is fear itself."

From FDR's first inaugural address,
March 4, 1933

"A democracy, the right kind of democracy, is bound together by the ties of neighborliness."

From FDR's speech to the Conference of Catholic Charities,
October 4, 1933

Important Dates in Franklin D. Roosevelt's Life

1882—Born on January 30 at Hyde Park, New York
1896—Starts at Groton School
1900—Enrolls at Harvard University
1905—Marries Anna Eleanor Roosevelt
1920—Runs for vice president and is defeated
1928—Elected governor of New York
1930—Re-elected governor of New York
1932—Elected president for his first term
1933—Inaugurated as president of the United States
1936—Re-elected president
1940—Re-elected president
1944—Re-elected president
1945—Dies at Warm Springs, Georgia; buried at Hyde Park

Words to Know

candidate—person who seeks an office
landslide—election in which one person does much better than another
front—an area where major fighting takes place
polio—contagious virus disease that damages the central nervous system, causing paralysis, loss of muscle tissue, and often death
politics—the art or science of governing
rationing—limiting the distribution of food or provisions. During World War II, meat, coffee, sugar, and rubber tires were rationed.
tutor—a private teacher

Read More

Devaney, John. *Franklin Delano Roosevelt, President.* New York: Walker, 1987.

Feinberg, Barbara. *Franklin D. Roosevelt: Gallant President.* New York: Lothrop, Lee & Shepard, 1981.

Freedman, Russell. *Franklin Delano Roosevelt.* New York: Clarion, 1990.

Osinski, Alice. *Franklin D. Roosevelt.* Chicago: Children's Press, 1987.

Useful Addresses and Internet Sites

Franklin D. Roosevelt Library
511 Albany Post Road
Hyde Park, NY 12538
library@roosevelt.nara.gov

Roosevelt Campobello International Park
P.O. Box 9
Welshpool, NB E0G 3H0
Canada

Franklin D. Roosevelt
http://www.academic.marist.edu/fdr/frank.html
White House for Kids
http://www.whitehouse.gov/WH/kids/html/kidshome.html

Index

Campobello Island, 13
Churchill, Winston, 19
fireside chats, 17
Great Depression, 5, 15, 17
Hyde Park, 5, 7, 21
New Deal, 17
polio, 13
Roosevelt,
  Anna Eleanor, 9
  James, 5
Sara Delano, 5
Teddy, 9, 11
Warm Springs, 13, 21
World War I, 11
World War II, 5, 19